PET CARE FOR KIDS

DOGS

BY KATHRYN STEVENS

The Child's World

Published by The Child's World®
1980 Lookout Drive • Mankato, MN 56003-1705
800-599-READ • www.childsworld.com

Acknowledgments
The Child's World®: Mary Berendes, Publishing Director
The Design Lab: Kathleen Petelinsek, Design and Page Production

Photo Credits: iStockphoto.com/André Weyer: 9; iStockphoto.com/
Craig Veltri: cover, back cover, 1, 3, 16, 20 (rag bone); iStockphoto.
com/Cristian Ardelean: 5; iStockphoto.com/Eric Isselée: cover
(Bernese, bichon, Dane), 1 (Bernese), 21 (Dane); iStockphoto.com/
Gaspare Messina: cover, back cover, 1, 3, 4 (bones); iStockphoto.
com/Gina Smith: 18; iStockphoto.com/Ivan Solis: 7; iStockphoto.
com/iztok noc: 11; iStockphoto.com/jclegg: cover, back cover, 1, 3,
4, 14, 16, 20 (leash, ball, tag); iStockphoto.com/Jeanne9: 12, 20
(brush); iStockphoto.com/Joseph C. Justice Jr.: 15; iStockphoto.
com/Justin Paget: 10; iStockphoto.com/Kristi Corbett: 6, 8 (treats);
iStockphoto.com/Luis Carlos Torres: cover, back cover, 1, 3, 6,
20 (dog dish); iStockphoto.com/Marcin Pikula: 21 (Chihuahua);
iStockphoto.com/Pamela Moore: 13; iStockphoto.com/Paul
Erickson: 17; iStockphoto.com/Rich Legg: 19; PhotoDisc: back
cover (Jack Russell), 4 (puppy), 22, 24

Library of Congress Cataloging-in-Publication Data
Stevens, Kathryn, 1954–
  Dogs / by Kathryn Stevens.
    p. cm. — (Pet care for kids)
  Includes index.
  ISBN 978-1-60253-181-9 (library bound : alk. paper)
  1. Dogs—Juvenile literature. I. Title. II. Series.
  SF426.5.S758 2009
  636.7—dc22   2008040000

Printed in the United States of America
Mankato, Minnesota
December, 2009
PA02038

NOTE TO PARENTS AND EDUCATORS

The Pet Care for Kids series is written for children who want to be part of the pet experience but are too young to be in charge of pets themselves. These books are intended to provide a kid-friendly supplement to more detailed information adults need to know about choosing and caring for different types of pets. They can help youngsters learn how to live happily with the animals in their lives, and, with adults' help and supervision, grow into responsible animal caretakers later on.

PET CARE FOR KIDS

CONTENTS

DOGS AS PETS

Dogs make great pets. And there are many dogs in need of good homes. But getting a dog is a big decision! It means planning ahead. Most dogs live for 10 or even 15 years. They need people who will take care of them for all that time.

▶ This Chihuahua is 15 years old. His family has cared for him the whole time.

▼ This bulldog puppy will grow into a large dog. His owners will take care of him for many years.

GOOD FOOD

Dogs need food that keeps them strong and healthy. Crunchy dried dog food is best for their teeth. Canned food is juicy and tasty. Dogs also love special dog treats. The treats are like doggie cookies! Dogs need plenty of clean water, too.

▶ Candy or cookies would not be good for this beagle. Dog treats are better for him.

▼ Dry dog food is good for dogs' teeth and gums.

TRAINING

Dogs need to learn good manners. They need to learn what they should and should not do. Gentle **training** works best. Yelling scares dogs, and hitting hurts them. But dogs love **praise** for doing things right!

▶ This young Labrador retriever is learning to sit and stay. The girl is saying "Good dog!" and giving him a treat.

Dogs are smart. They can learn all kinds of things. They can learn to behave around people or other animals. You can teach them to come when called. They can learn great tricks, too. Training dogs can be lots of fun!

▶ This border collie has learned **agility**. She zigzags between poles. She is having fun!

◀ This labrador retriever has learned how to shake hands.

GOOD HEALTH

Dogs need trips to the animal doctor, or **vet**. They need shots to keep from getting sick. They need to have their toenails cut. They need **grooming** to keep their fur clean. Baths and brushing help. Some dogs even get haircuts!

▶ A vet is listening to this Chihuahua's heart.

◀ Some dog brushes have two sides. One side is for tangles. The other side is for smoothing the fur.

SAFETY

Dogs trust their owners to keep them safe. Fenced-in yards help keep dogs out of danger. In other places, a leash is a good idea. Dog tags can help lost dogs get home. Other people can read the tags. The tags tell them where the dogs live.

▶ This Labrador retriever is having a great time! She is playing in her family's fenced yard.

◀ Leashes and name tags help keep dogs safe.

PLAYTIME

Just like kids, dogs love to play. Playing keeps dogs happy and healthy.

Dogs like toys they can chew. They like chasing and catching balls. Many dogs love to play fetch. They have fun doing other tricks, too.

▶ This golden retriever is playing fetch— in the water!

◀ There are lots of fun toys made just for dogs.

LOTS OF LOVE!

Dogs get lonely being by themselves. They want to be part of a group. They love being part of a family. They like to be petted. They like gentle cuddling. They want to be best friends!

▸ This golden retriever loves being with her family!

▾ This girl and her Labrador retriever are best friends.

NEEDS:

* good food
* clean water
* leash, collar, and tags
* exercise
* toys
* grooming
* visits to the vet
* training and praise

DANGERS:

* chocolate, grapes, or raisins
* household poisons
* traffic on the street
* eating trash
* getting too hot or too cold

EARS:
Dogs have very good hearing.

BIG DOGS:
Great Danes can be 40 inches (about 1 meter) tall at the shoulder.

NOSE:
Dogs have a much better sense of smell than people do.

SMALL DOGS:
Some Chihuahuas are only 6 inches (15 centimeters) tall at the shoulder.

SPEED:
Some dogs can reach speeds of over 40 miles (64 kilometers) an hour.

GLOSSARY

agility *(uh-JIH-luh-tee)* Agility is being able to move quickly and easily.

grooming *(GROO-ming)* Grooming an animal is cleaning and brushing it.

praise *(PRAYZ)* To praise a dog is to say it did something well.

training *(TRAY-ning)* Training an animal means teaching it what to do.

vet *(VET)* A vet is a doctor who takes care of animals. Vet is short for "veterinarian" *(vet-rih-NAYR-ee-un)*.

TO FIND OUT MORE

Books:

Evans, Mark. *Puppy*. New York: Dorling Kindersley, 2001.

Roca, Núria, and Rosa Curto. *Our New Dog*. Hauppauge, NY: Barron's Educational Series, 2006.

Royston, Angela. *Puppy*. New York: Dorling Kindersley, 2007.

Video/DVD:

Paws, Claws, Feathers & Fins: A Kid's Guide to Happy, Healthy Pets. Goldhil Learning Series (Video 1993, DVD 2005).

Web Sites:

Visit our Web page for lots of links about pet care:
http://www.childsworld.com/links

Note to parents, teachers, and librarians: We routinely verify our Web links to make sure they are safe, active sites—so encourage your readers to check them out!

INDEX

ABOUT THE AUTHOR

Kathryn Stevens has authored and edited many books for young readers, including books on animals ranging from grizzly bears to fleas. She's a lifelong pet-lover and currently cares for a big, huggable pet-therapy dog named Fudge.